THE PALEO SLOWCOOKER DIET COOKBOOK

80+ Mouthwatering, Healthy Paleo Recipes for Busy Mom and Dad: A Gluten and Diary Free Cookbook.

By

MARY CARTER

THE PALEO SLOWCOOKER DIET COOKBOOK

Copyright © 2019, By: MARY CARTER

ISBN-13: 978-1-950772-44-5
ISBN-10: 1-950772-44-6

All Rights Reserved. No part of this publication may be reproduced in any form or by any means, including scanning, photocopying, or otherwise without prior written permission of the copyright holder.

Disclaimer:

The information provided in this book is designed to provide helpful information on the subjects discussed. The publisher and author are not responsible for any specific health or allergy needs that may require medical supervision and are not liable for any damages or negative consequences from any treatment, action, application or

THE PALEO SLOWCOOKER DIET COOKBOOK

Table of Contents

INTRODUCTION 7
    LIVING A HEALTHY AND WEALTHY PALEOLITHIC LIFESTYLE 7
THE PALEO DIET FOR A HEALTHY AND WEALTHY FAMILY 8
    Crockpot Bean Stew 8
    Crockpot Veggies in a Bag 9
    Crockpot Chicken with Apple and Sweet Potato 10
    Crockpot Chicken and Veggie Delight 11
    Crockpot Bacon Cheese Potatoes 12
    Crockpot Applesauce 13
    Slow Cooked Bacon-Wrapped Chicken 14
    Slow Cooker Cajun Beef Chili 15
    Spicy Mustard Crockpot Chicken 16
    Italian Style Chuck Roast 17
    Cranberry Juice made in a Crock Pot 18
    Crock Pot Rump Roast 19
    Peach Pie Crock Pot Oatmeal 20
    Cherry Pie Crock Pot Oatmeal (Soaked & Gluten-Free) 21
    Scalloped Potatoes & Bacon (Crockpot) 22
    Slow Cooker Bean less Chili (gluten-free, ... 23
    Crockpot Turkey Chili 24
    Potato Ham Chowder 25
    Paleo Thai Soup 26
    Crockpot Brownie Bites 27
    Easy Butternut Squash Soup 28
    CROCKPOT PINTO BEANS 29
    Crockpot Refried Beans 30
    Moroccan-Style Slow Cooked Lamb 31

THE PALEO SLOWCOOKER DIET COOKBOOK

Crockpot Sausage and Cabbage 32
Easiest Crock Pot Taco Meat 33
Slow Cooker Beef with Nettles & Astragalus 34
Crock-Pot Swedish Meatballs 35
Slow cooker Beef brisket 37
Buffalo Chicken Lettuce Wraps (Gluten Free 38
Paleo Beef Short Ribs 39
Crock-Pot Chicken Fajitas 40
CHICKEN PUMPKIN SOUP 41
HERB-ROASTED CHICKEN WITH VEGETABLES 43
Slow Cooker Chicken and Potato Soup 45
Slow Cooker Cranberry Sauce 46
Creamy Paleo Cashew Curry Cauliflower 47
Paleo Kielbasa & Super Kraut Recipe 48
SLOW COOKER VINDALOO WITH BEEF, PORK, CHICKEN, GOAT, OR LAMB 49
Asian Slow Cooked Pork 51
Healing Cuisine BBQ Meatballs 53
Chicken Hearts Stroganoff (Slow Cooker Version) 54
CROCK POT CASHEW CHICKEN 56
Crockpot Chicken de Provence 57
Slow Cooker Apricot Chicken 58
Slow Cooker Creamy Italian Chicken 60
CROCK POT SWISS STEAK 61
Slow-Cooker Korean-Style Beef Short Ribs 63
Roasted Red Pepper Sweet Potato Soup 64
Slow Cooker Super-Fast Meatloaf 65
Slow Cooker Chicken Roll-Ups with Prosciutto and Asparagus 67
Paleo Refried Beans (Delicata Squash) 68

THE PALEO SLOWCOOKER DIET COOKBOOK

- Super Easy Crock Pot Spaghetti Squash Curry 69
- Slow Cooker Red & Yellow Pepper 71
- Cinnamon & Cayenne Sweet Potatoes and Apples 73
- Saratoga Chips 74
- Easy Crock Pot "Rotisserie Style" Chicken 75
- Crockpot Chicken Tacos 77
- Crock Pot Roasted Chicken Recipe 79
- Easy Slow Cooker Cuban Ropa Viejas 80
- Savory Slow Cooker Chuck Roast & Butternut Squash Combo Meal 82
- Coconut milk curry beef stew crock pot recipe 83
- Rosemary Lemon Garlic Lamb with Sweet Potato Noodles 85
- Apple Cranberry Mulled Cider (Slow-Cooked) 87
- Crock-Pot Chicken Tortilla Soup 89
- Coconut Green Chili Chicken Soup (dairy and gluten free) 90
- Slow Cooker Baked Apple Recipe 92
- Homemade Slow Cooker Hot Chocolate 93
- Best BBQ Crock Pot Chicken 94
- Crock Pot Balsamic Roast 95
- Slow Cook Thai Chicken 97
- Italian Crock Pot Chili 99
- Slow-Cooker Barbecue Ribs Recipe 101
- Slow Cooker Queso Chicken Chili Recipe 103
- Slow Cooker Buffalo Chicken Meatballs Recipe 104
- Slow Cooker Chipotle Barbacoa Brisket 105
- Slow cooked pork ribs recipe 107
- Sour Cream & Bacon Crock Pot Chicken 108
- Crockpot Breakfast Casserole 109
- Casein -Free Crockpot Frito Pie (Gluten –Free) 111

Crockpot Pear, Apple and Pork Dinner 113
Conclusion 114

INTRODUCTION

LIVING A HEALTHY AND WEALTHY PALEOLITHIC LIFESTYLE

If you live a Paleolithic lifestyle, your body will gradually burn fat naturally for life. If you wish to slim down, and live a healthier lifestyle Paleo is your sure answer. The advantage about a Paleo diet plan is that it provides necessary nutrients and vitamins your body needs to drop weight and keep it off for the rest of your life.

It will make you look much younger than your friends of the same age range. You will not only get highly healthy foods concepts, but also foods high in anti-oxidants that will certainly assist in eliminating free radicals and minimize inflammation. So give your cells the right fuel and they will do the rest.

The Paleo diet consists of organic foods devoid of chemicals and other damaging elements that will aid your food digestion process your immune system reacts well and your gut relaxes.

If you live a Paleolithic lifestyle, you will experience a boost in energy. However, Paleo diets are excellent sources of quality protein, which leads to a boost in energy.

As pointed out earlier Paleo diet helps boost your immune system response, decreased swelling, get rid of damaging toxins and lower inflammation which is the root cause of numerous degenerative conditions.

THE PALEO DIET FOR A HEALTHY AND WEALTHY FAMILY

Crockpot Bean Stew

Ingredients

1 cup of dry beans (picked over and rinsed)

1 small onion (finely chopped)

3 tablespoons of uncooked white rice

1 teaspoon of dried thyme

1/8 Teaspoon of ground white or black pepper

6 cups of chicken broth (or vegetable broth)

2 medium carrots (peeled and finely diced)

2 celery stalks (finely diced)

2 tablespoons of minced garlic

1/2 teaspoon of salt

Directions:

First, you add the entire ingredients to a Crockpot and cook on low for about 6 - 8 hours.

Crockpot Veggies in a Bag

Ingredients

2 Chopped Yellow Squash

2 Chopped Green Pepper

2 Tablespoons of Fresh Basil

2-Chopped Onion

12 – 16 Chopped Red Potatoes

4 teaspoons of Minced Garlic

Directions:

1. First, you put all ingredients in a Gallon Freezer Size Bag.

2. When you are ready to cook, I suggest you cook the veggies by themselves in the Crockpot on low for about 6 hours.

3. You may serve either alone or with meat.

Crockpot Chicken with Apple and Sweet Potato

Ingredients

2 pounds of boneless, skinless chicken breasts (cut into 1-inch cubes)

4 cloves of garlic (finely minced)

2 cups of unsweetened applesauce

1 teaspoon of ground ginger

4 sweet potatoes (peeled and cut into 1 - inch chunks)

Sea salt plus cracked black pepper

1 cup of chopped red onion

4 teaspoons of apple cider vinegar

2 tablespoons of curry powder (feel free to use cumin if you do not have curry)

Directions:

1. First, you layer the sweet potato chunks and chicken breasts in the bottom of a slow cooker.

2. After which you season with salt and pepper.

3. After that, you stir together the garlic, red onion, applesauce, cider vinegar, curry powder, and ginger.

4. At this point, you pour the mixture over the chicken and sweet potato chunks.

5. Then you cover and cook on low for about 6 - 8 hours, until the chicken and sweet potatoes are tender.

6. When serving, I suggest you serve alone or over rice.

Crockpot Chicken and Veggie Delight

Ingredients

8 chicken breasts

2 (32oz.) Cans of Die Fratelli Tomato Sauce

Variety of Veggies, cut up such as Zucchini, Mushroom, Onion, Peppers (you should use whatever your family likes

Directions:

1. First, you place chicken in Crockpot.

2. After which you add veggies, tomato sauce, Basil, Oregano (preferably, fresh) and water if necessary to cover.

3. After that, you cook on high heat for 1 hour and turn down too low for 3 hours.

4. Finally, you enjoy over a bed of rice

Crockpot Bacon Cheese Potatoes

Tips:

Make sure you did not use as much onion, if you using green onions.

Ingredients

2 small onions (thinly sliced)

1 pound of cheddar cheese, thinly sliced (shredded is fine)

Butter

1 green Onions (it is optional)

½ pound of bacon, diced (I suggest you bake it first in the oven so that it is " done" and browned then you dice it and place in the crock pot).

12 - 16 red potatoes, quartered (if you using regular potatoes you slice thinly or if you use a new potato then halve)

Salt and pepper, to taste

Directions:

1. First, you line Crockpot with foil, leaving enough to cover the potatoes when finished (this will help it not to stick and to steam the potatoes).

2. After which you layer half each of the bacon, onions, potatoes and cheese in Crockpot.

3. After that, you season to taste with salt and pepper and dot with (real) butter.

4. At this point, you repeat layers of bacon, onions, potatoes and cheese.

5. Make sure you dot with butter.

6. At this point, you cover with the remaining foil.

7. Finally, you cover and cook on low for about 4 - 6 hours.

Crockpot Applesauce

Ingredients

2 strips of lemon peel

10 teaspoons of light brown sugar (unpacked)

16 medium apples (use a variety)

2 teaspoons of fresh lemon juice

6 inches' cinnamon stick

Directions:

1. First, you peel, core and chop apples and place in Crockpot.

2. After which you add lemon peel, lemon juice, brown sugar and cinnamon stick.

3. After that, you set Crockpot to low and cook for about 6 hours.

4. At this point, you stir occasionally (apples will slowly become applesauce).

5. Finally, you remove cinnamon stick and blend.

Slow Cooked Bacon-Wrapped Chicken

Ingredients

3 cups of homemade BBQ sauce

8 apples (peeled and chopped)

16 to 24 slices bacon

8 boneless skinless chicken breasts

4 tablespoons of fresh lemon juice

2 onions (diced)

Directions:

1. First, you wrap each chicken breast with bacon slices.

2. After which you place each bacon-wrapped chicken breast in your slow cooker.

3. After that, you combine the BBQ sauce, lemon juice, apples, and onions in a bowl, and mix thoroughly.

4. At this point, you pour the BBQ sauce mixture over the chicken.

5. Then you cover and cook on low for about 6 to 8 hours.

6. Finally, you serve the chicken breasts topped with the apple and onion mixture.

Slow Cooker Cajun Beef Chili

Ingredients

1 teaspoon of Cajun seasoning

1 large onions (chopped)

4 cloves garlic (minced)

2 cups of beef broth (organic if Paleo)

2 lbs. of beef stew meat

½ teaspoon of pepper

1 green bell pepper (chopped)

2 cans of diced tomatoes (14 oz.)

Directions

1. First, you sprinkle beef evenly with Cajun seasoning and pepper.

2. After which you combine onion, bell pepper and garlic in a greased slow cooker.

3. After that, you place beef on top of the vegetables and top the beef with the diced tomatoes.

4. At this point, you pour beef broth over top of everything and replace the lid.

5. Finally, you cook on LOW for about 4-6 hours.

Spicy Mustard Crockpot Chicken

Ingredients:

2 tablespoons of olive oil

½ teaspoon of sea salt

2/3 cup of chicken broth

3 tablespoons of Dijon mustard

1 tablespoon of paleo chili garlic sauce, here (feel free to half the recipe)

4 chicken breasts

1 teaspoon of garlic powder

½ teaspoon of pepper

4 tablespoons of honey

3 tablespoons of stone ground mustard

Directions:

1. First, you mix the entire ingredients except chicken in a small bowl.

2. After which you place chicken in the bottom of the Crockpot and pour sauce over it.

3. After that, you cook on low for about 3 hours.

4. At this point, you remove chicken and pour sauce into a small saucepot.

5. Then you heat sauce over medium to a simmer for about 10 minutes.

6. Finally, you serve chicken with sauce on top.

Italian Style Chuck Roast

Ingredients

32 ounces of diced tomatoes (canned)

12 ounces of tomato sauce

1 onion (chopped)

2 stalks celery (sliced)

1 tablespoon of thyme

Four bay leaves

One large chuck roast

12 ounces of tomato paste

Eight cloves garlic (minced)

4 carrots (peeled and chopped)

1 tablespoon of oregano

2 teaspoons of salt

2 teaspoons of black pepper

Directions:

1. First, you mix the entire ingredients except for your roast and stir well.

2. After which you cut your chuck roast into small pieces, as for me I prefer to cut each one into three pieces and then place in the bottom of the crock-pot.

3. After that, you pour all of your sauce over your roast and cover.

4. At this point, you cook on low for about 8-10 hours or high for 4-5 hours.

5. Then you serve.

Note: remember to save the left over sauce and use it on your eggs, meatballs, chicken, spaghetti squash etc.

Cranberry Juice made in a Crock Pot

Ingredients

4 oranges (freshly squeezed)

2 lbs. of fresh cranberries

16 cups of water

Sweeten to taste (I prefer to use ½ cup local raw honey, but when it unavailable feel free to substitute with Organic Raw Honey)

Cinnamon stick (it is optional)

Garnish with mint (it is optional)

Directions:

1. First, you wash your cranberries and put them in a Crockpot along with your freshly squeezed orange juice.

2. After which you fill the crock-pot with water, enough that it will barely cover the berries.

3. Then you cook on high for about 4-5 hours.

4. After that, you strain the liquid from the berries and then put into a pitcher.

5. Then you add sweetener of your choice and allow the juice to cool then cover and refrigerate until cold.

6. Finally, you add some alcohol if you would like.

Crock Pot Rump Roast

Ingredients

2 onions (diced)

2 tablespoons of paprika

1 teaspoon of cayenne

1 cup of organic beef stock

2 grass fed rump roast

2 tablespoons of black pepper

4 teaspoons of chili powder

1 teaspoon of garlic

½ teaspoon of mustard powder

Directions:

1. First, you combine the entire spices above and mix well.

2. After which you generously rub this spice mixture all over your rump roast to your taste liking and if you do not like too many spices, I will suggest you just lightly coat it.

3. After that, you line the bottom of your crock-pot with your diced onions.

4. At this point, you place your seasoned roast on top.

5. Then you pour in your beef stock, cover and cook on low for about 10 hours.

Peach Pie Crock Pot Oatmeal

Ingredients

1 cup of rye flakes or ground buckwheat grouts (it is optional)

2 cups of raw milk (or coconut milk)

2 tablespoons of raw apple cider vinegar

2 cups of organic peaches (raw, frozen or preserved)

1 teaspoon of ground cardamom

2 teaspoons of vanilla extract

4 cups of steel cut oats (preferably, gluten-free)

6 cups of filtered water

½ cup (8 TBS) pastured butter or coconut oil

½ cup of raw honey (or grade B maple syrup)

3 teaspoons of ground cinnamon

4 tablespoons of chia seeds

1 teaspoon of salt (I prefer Real Salt)

Directions:

1. First, in the morning before you want your oatmeal, you butter (or coconut oil) the bottom of a small crock-pot and add oats, water and apple cider vinegar.

2. After which you allow to soak for the entire day (Do not drain).

3. In the evening before you go to bed, you add the remaining ingredients.

4. After which you mix and turn crock-pot on low.

5. Then you cook overnight for about 7-8 hours.

6. Finally, when serving, you serve with extra honey, maple syrup, milk, or coconut milk if desired.

Cherry Pie Crock Pot Oatmeal (Soaked & Gluten-Free)

Ingredients

6 cups of filtered water

2 cups of milk (preferably raw) or coconut milk

4 teaspoons of vanilla extract (or almond extract)

4 tablespoons of chia seeds (it is optional)

2 cups of organic cherries (feel free to use fresh or frozen cherries that have been thawed or rehydrated dried cherries)

4 cups of gluten-free steel cut oats

2 tablespoons of raw apple cider vinegar

½ cup of butter, ghee, or coconut oil

1teaspoon of real salt

½ cup of raw honey

Directions:

1. First, you butter or grease the bottom of a small crock-pot and add water, oats and apple cider vinegar.

2. After which you allow to soak all day (Do not drain).

3. After that, you add remaining ingredients and stir.

4. Then you cook overnight in crock-pot on low.

5. Finally, you serve with milk or coconut milk, extra butter and honey or maple syrup.

Scalloped Potatoes & Bacon (Crockpot)

Ingredients

2 cups of shredded Cheddar cheese

6 cloves garlic (crushed)

5 cups of milk (I prefer whole milk)

Salt & Pepper to taste

6 pounds' potatoes (peeled and thinly sliced)

1cup of chopped onion

2 cups of chopped cooked bacon

6 Tablespoons of flour

3 tablespoons of Better than Bouillon Organic Mushroom Base

Directions:

1. First, you grease the Crockpot.

2. After which you mix potatoes, onions, and garlic and pour in Crockpot.

3. After that, you whisk over low heat milk, bouillon base, and flour until the mixture thickens.

4. At this point, you pour milk mixture over potatoes, add bacon, and top with cheese.

5. Then you cook on low for about 7-8 hours or high for 4-5 hours.

Slow Cooker Bean less Chili (gluten-free,

Ingredients

4 cans (28 ounces total) stewed tomatoes, undrained

2 small white onions (chopped)

2 can (4 ounces) chopped green chilies

2-garlic clove (minced)

½ teaspoon of ground pepper

2 to 3 pounds of ground beef

2 can (8 ounces) tomato sauce

2 medium green peppers (chopped)

2 tablespoons of chili powder

2 teaspoons of regular (or Himalayan salt)

1teaspoon of paprika

Toppings such as the shredded cheddar cheese, sliced green onions, sour cream, and pickled jalapenos slice.

Directions

1. First, you crumble beef into slow cooker.

2. After which you add the next 10 ingredients and mix thoroughly.

3. After that, you cover and cook on high for about 4-6 hours or until meat is no longer pink.

4. Then you are free to serve with toppings of your choice.

Crockpot Turkey Chili

Ingredients:

4 Onions (diced)

8 cloves of Garlic

2 can Tomato Sauce (it is about 30 oz.)

2 teaspoons of Chili Powder or more if you like it hot.

6 pounds of Turkey or the meat/combo of your choice (cooked and diced or shredded)

10 Carrots (diced)

8 cans Diced Tomatoes

4 tablespoons of Cumin

Directions:

1. First, you dump the entire ingredients in your Crockpot.

2. After which you stir and cover.

3. After that, you put your crock-pot on high for about 4 hrs. or low for 8 hours.

4. Finally, you topped your chili with a dollop of guacamole that is if you desire.

Potato Ham Chowder

Ingredients

2 cups of cubed ham steak

6 cups of chicken broth

4-6 cloves garlic (chopped)

½ teaspoon of black pepper

8 cups of potatoes (peeled and diced)

2 cups of onions (chopped)

4 cups of heavy cream

2 teaspoons of unrefined sea salt

Directions:

1. First, you place the entire ingredients in slow cooker except heavy cream.

2. After which you cook on low for about 6-7 hours.

3. After that, you add heavy cream.

4. Then you cook for an additional hour.

5. Finally, you top with cheese, green onions, chives, bacon or any one that fits your fancy.

Paleo Thai Soup

Ingredients

2 cups of coconut milk (from can)

4 cups of cooked cubed/shredded chicken

4 tablespoons of Thai red curry paste (you can add more if you like 'spicy')

2 teaspoons of fresh grated ginger

12 cups of chicken broth

4 limes, juice

2 cups of pea-pods (cut the ends off)

4 tablespoons of Thai fish sauce

Directions:

1. First, you place chicken broth, coconut milk, lime juice, ginger, Thai paste, fish sauce in crock-pot, and whisk together.

2. After which you add in chicken and pea-pods.

3. Then you cook on low for about 5-6 hours or high for 2-3.

Note:

If pea-pods are not in season, feel free to substitute it with broccoli.

Crockpot Brownie Bites

Ingredients

2 cups of coconut sugar (or preferably other granulated sugar of your choice)

4 teaspoons of baking powder

2 teaspoons of salt

1cup of full fat (or unsweetened coconut milk)

2/3 cup of brewed coffee or water

4 cups of almond flour

1 ¼ cups of unsweetened cocoa powder

4 teaspoons of baking soda

4 eggs

1cup of butter or coconut oil, melted

4 teaspoons of pure vanilla extract

Directions:

1. First, you grease the Crockpot with coconut oil.

2. After which you mix the entire ingredients and spread evenly into the Crockpot.

3. After that, you cook on low for about 4-5 hours and once the brownies are cooked through, let cool for about ½ an hour.

4. Then you scoop out with a cookie scoop or large spoon and form into balls.

5. Finally, you drizzle with my homemade caramel glaze (for an over-the-top dessert).

Easy Butternut Squash Soup

Ingredients:

2 cans of full-fat coconut milk (or equivalent amount of homemade coconut milk)

2 apples, peeled (and cut into chunks)

1 teaspoon of ginger

2 large butternut squash (peeled and cubed)

2 cups of chicken broth

4 teaspoons of cinnamon

2 teaspoons of nutmeg

Directions:

1. First, you place the entire ingredients in slow cooker and set to Low.

2. After which you allow to cook for about 6 to 8 hours.

3. At this point when squash is soft, you blend soup with an immersion blender or carefully transfer to a blender to process until it is smooth and silky.

4. After that, you season with unrefined sea salt and pepper.

5. Finally, you top with a swirl of olive oil or dollop of sour cream (if you can tolerate dairy).

CROCKPOT PINTO BEANS

INGREDIENTS

12 cups water (or broth)

Pepper to taste

2 bay leaves (only if you vegetarian)

2 lbs. of dry pinto beans

2-1 teaspoons of sea salt (add more if need be)

2 tablespoons of bacon fat or 4 pieces of bacon, or a ham hock (omit if you vegetarian)

Directions:

1. First, you rinse and sort beans.

2. Then in a pot or bowl, you add warm water covering the beans by two inches.

3. After which you let soak overnight.

4. After that, you drain the next day and add beans to a Crockpot.

5. Then you add 12 cups of water or broth as well as fat (use a bay leaf if you are vegetarian).

6. At this point, you cook on low for about 7-9 hours or on high for 4-5 hours.

7. Finally, after beans are tender, you add salt and pepper to taste.

Crockpot Refried Beans

Tips:

It makes many beans, but the leftovers freeze well.

Ingredients:

2 small onions

2 Jalapeño

6 cups of water

1 teaspoon of salt

8 cup dry pinto beans

8 garlic cloves

4 cups of bone broth

2 teaspoons of paprika

2 teaspoons of coriander

Directions:

1. First, you put the dry pinto beans in the Crockpot and cover generously with water.

2. After which you let them soak overnight and drain the water, in the morning.

3. After that, you put the beans back in the pot with a small chopped onion, the garlic, Jalapeño, bone broth and water.

4. At this point, you cook on high for about 6 hours.

5. At a point when the beans are done cooking, you add the paprika, coriander, and salt.

6. Then you mash them with an immersion blender or even a hand mixer.

7. Finally, you serve hot with cheese or sour cream.

Moroccan-Style Slow Cooked Lamb

Ingredients:

6 teaspoons of ground cumin

2 teaspoons of ground ginger

2 teaspoons of turmeric

2 teaspoons of sumac or grated lemon zest

2-lamb shoulder or 8 lambs chop (preferably, shoulder or loin)

2 teaspoons of ground cinnamon

2 teaspoons of chili flakes

1teaspoon of garlic salt

2 teaspoons of ground coriander

Directions:

1. First, you combined the entire ingredients except the lamb in a large bowl.

2. After which you rub all over the lamb and leave to marinate for at least an hour, preferably overnight.

3. In the other way round, you can throw it all in a pinch without marinating, and it will still be tasty.

4. After that, you place in the slow cooker and cook on low for around 8 hours or high for around four hours.

5. At this point, the lamb should be tender, if it is not, cook it a little longer.

6. Make sure you serve with quinoa, rice pilaf, roast veggies or salad.

Crockpot Sausage and Cabbage

Ingredients

2 large onions (coarsely chopped)

2 cups of apple juice or water works just as well

4-6 large potatoes (diced)

Salt and pepper to taste

2 small head cabbage (coarsely shredded)

3 to 4 pounds of kielbasa

2 tablespoons of Dijon mustard

4-6 large carrots (diced)

2 tablespoons of cider vinegar

Directions:

1. First, you layer the cabbage, onion, potatoes, carrots, and sausage in a Crockpot.

2. After which you whisk together the juice, vinegar, mustard and pour over Crockpot ingredients.

3. After that, you cover and cook on low for about 8 to 10 hours depending on your Crockpot.

4. I once cooked it on high for about an hour and then on low for about 3-4 hours when I forget to get it ready earlier in the day.

Easiest Crock Pot Taco Meat

Ingredients

2 large onions (finely minced)

2 cups of strained tomatoes (or tomato sauce)

12 tablespoons of taco seasoning (or Mexican seasoning)

3 teaspoons of garlic powder

2 teaspoons of cumin

2 teaspoons of sea salt

8 pounds grass-fed ground beef or ground bison (or preferably a mix of the two)

20 cloves garlic (finely minced)

½ cup of gluten-free Worcestershire

2 jalapenos (finely minced)

3 teaspoons of onion powder

2 teaspoons of coriander

Directions:

1. First, you place the entire ingredients in a slow cooker and stir together well.

2. After which you cook on low for about 6-10 hours, stirring every once in a while if convenient.

3. This recipe makes delicious tacos, burritos, taco salads, quesadillas, and much more.

4. Note that this taco meat freezes fantastically and makes fast and delicious dinners.

Slow Cooker Beef with Nettles & Astragalus

Ingredients:

½ to 1 cup of dried nettle leaf

2 (28 ounce) can or jar of tomatoes (if you are using canned, make sure the lining of the can is BPA free)

8 to 12 or more cloves of garlic (minced or 2 tablespoons dried)

8 to 12 potatoes, yams (sweet potatoes or a mix)

2 teaspoons of thyme

Fresh herbs (or greens to go on top if you desire)

5 to 6 pounds of beef stew meat, grass-fed & organic if need be

8 to 16 slices of astragalus root

2 large onions (chopped)

12 to 16 carrots

4 to 6 bay leaves

Salt and pepper, to taste

Directions:

1. First, you place the stew meat in your slow cooker and start layering the ingredients on top.

2. As for me, I did not cut up the carrots and potatoes, I just let them cook whole, and this makes it so easy.

3. After which you cook on low for about 8 hours and serve.

Crock-Pot Swedish Meatballs

Ingredients:

½ cup of beef stock, milk or cream

2 eggs, beaten

3 teaspoons of salt

¼ teaspoons of allspice

6-10 Tablespoons of tallow, coconut oil, ghee or butter

4 cups of beef stock

1 cup of gluten-free bread crumbs

2 lbs. of ground beef

1 onion (chopped fine or grated)

½ teaspoon of pepper

Dashes of nutmeg

4 Tablespoons of gluten-free flour of your choice

Directions:

1. First, you combine the breadcrumbs and ½-cup stock in a large bowl.

2. After which you allow to soak for about 5 minutes and drain any excess moisture.

3. After that, you add the ground beef, egg, onion and 2 teaspoons of salt, ¼ teaspoon of pepper, allspice and nutmeg.

4. Then you mix well and shape into meatballs.

5. At this point, you melt the fat in a skillet over medium-high heat.

6. Furthermore, you brown the meatballs in batches and transfer to a slow cooker.

7. After which you whisk the flour into the skillet and cook until slightly browned.

8. After that, you whisk in the stock and remaining salt and pepper.

9. Then you pour over the meatballs, cover and cook on low for about 6 hours.

10. Finally, you serve with sautéed greens and rice or mashed potatoes.

Slow cooker Beef brisket

Ingredients

3-4 cups of orange juice

4 lbs. of beef brisket

2 teaspoons of black pepper

2 small Fuji apples (it is optional)

4 tablespoons of tomato paste

4 medium sized yellow onions

4 teaspoons of sea salt

2 teaspoons of Saigon cinnamon (it is optional)

Directions:

1. First, you put brisket on bottom of slow cooker.

2. After which you add in the ingredients.

3. After that, you set slow cooker on high for an hour, just to get the heat going.

4. Then you convert slow cooker too low to 7-8 hours.

5. Finally, you add more sea salt or black pepper to taste.

Buffalo Chicken Lettuce Wraps (Gluten Free

Ingredients:

3 cups of Buffalo Sauce (ensure GFDF)

16 lettuce leaves

6 pounds of chicken, boneless skinless breasts

2-ounce dry Ranch dressing mix (GFDF) or rather you make your own

Directions:

1. First, you combine the entire ingredients in slow cooker.

2. After which you cook on high for about 3-4 hours or on low for 5-6 hours.

3. After that, you remove chicken, shred, and then mix to combine.

4. Then you serve in a lettuce leaf.

Directions for freezing:

1. You start by following the above slow cooker directions and let meat mixture cool.

2. After which you divide among indicated number of freezer bags.

3. After that, you remove as much air as possible, then label & seal.

IF YOU WANT TO SERVE:

1. You first thaw and then you reheat chicken mixture until heated through.

2. Then you scoop into a lettuce leaf and enjoy.

Paleo Beef Short Ribs

Ingredients

10 cups of red wine

2 onions (thinly sliced)

2-4lbs grass fed beef short ribs

2 cups of mushrooms

Directions

1. First, you sear the beef in a skillet on medium heat for about 2 mins on each side.

2. After which you place the entire ingredients in the crock-pot on low for about 11 hours.

Crock-Pot Chicken Fajitas

Ingredients:

2-4 onions (sliced)

2 red bell pepper (cut in strips)

4 cloves garlic (pressed)

2 teaspoons of chili powder

½ cup of chicken stock or water

4-8 boneless, skinless chicken breasts (cut into strips)

2 green bell pepper (cut in strips)

2 jalapeno pepper, chopped (it is optional)

2 teaspoons of salt

2 teaspoons of cumin

4-6 fresh tomatoes (diced or 2 (14½–ounce) can diced tomatoes

Ingredients:

1. First, you combine the entire ingredients in a crock-pot and cook on low for about 6-8 hours.

2. After which you shred the chicken and return to the crock-pot before serving.

3. When serving, I suggest you serve over rice or on tortillas with salsa, with refried beans and a salad on the side.

CHICKEN PUMPKIN SOUP

INGREDIENTS

2 lbs. Free Range Chicken Breast, cubed

1 Yellow onion

4 cups of Chicken Broth

2 (16 oz.) can of Pumpkin (or freshly pureed)

1 cup Half & Half

4 sprigs of fresh Rosemary

10 medium sized Basil Leaves

Salt and Pepper to taste

1 cup of Ghee (or Grass Fed Butter)

6 cloves of Garlic

2 tablespoons of Honey

1 cup of Water

4 cups of cubed Pumpkin or Yams

10 leaves of fresh Pineapple Sage

2 teaspoons of fresh Thyme

2 teaspoons of Cinnamon

2 teaspoons of Cayenne Pepper

Directions:

1. First, you use a Dutch oven to heat ghee/butter over a medium heat.

2. At a point when the ghee/butter melts, you add in the cubed pumpkin and chicken.

3. After which you cook until almost half way done and chicken is white all around and pink inside.

4. After that, you pour in the remaining ingredients, except half- &-half, and turn the heat up to medium high.

5. Then once the soup is at a boil, you bring it down to a simmer and cover for approximately 15-20 minutes.

6. Finally, you pour in half- &-half, mix and serve.

HERB-ROASTED CHICKEN WITH VEGETABLES

INGREDIENTS

4-8 sweet potatoes (or yams)

8 or more stalks of celery

2-4 large onions

Ghee

Juice of 1 lemon

Rosemary (preferably, dried or fresh)

Sea salt

2 free-range (organic chicken)

8-12 potatoes

8 or more carrots

2 heads of garlic (peeled)

Thyme (preferably, dried or fresh)

Herb mare

Freshly ground pepper, to taste

Directions:

1. First, you rinse chicken and pat dry.

2. After which you place in roasting pan and rub ghee over the breast and legs.

3. After that, you squeeze lemon juice over chicken.

4. Then you arrange chopped vegetables all around chicken and season everything with herb mare, salt, pepper, thyme, and rosemary.

5. At this point, you roast covered in oven for 1½ hours or longer depending on weight of the chicken.

6. Finally, you serve with garlic bread.

Slow Cooker Chicken and Potato Soup

Ingredients

4 cups of potatoes (diced)

2 cups of carrots (chopped)

2 teaspoons of Herbs de Province

4-6 cloves garlic (minced)

2 lbs. boneless, skinless chicken thighs

2 cups of celery (chopped)

1 cup of onion (chopped)

2 teaspoons of unrefined sea salt

8 cups of homemade chicken stock (or bone broth)

Directions:

First, you put the entire ingredients into slow cooker and cook on low for about 7-8 hours or high for 4-5.

Slow Cooker Cranberry Sauce

Ingredients:

2 medium Bartlett pear (cored and diced smaller than the cranberries)

2 tablespoons of freshly grated ginger

½ cup of coconut sap crystals

2 (14 ounce) of bag of cranberries

Juice and zest of 2 medium orange

½ cup of raw honey

Directions:

1. First, you wash your cranberries and strain excess water off before dumping into your slow cooker.

2. After which you add your pear, orange juice, orange zest, and ginger, then you stir.

3. After that, you add your honey and coconut crystals and try your best to stir evenly. If clumps form, I suggest you set them towards the top.

4. At this point, you leave your lid slightly cracked to allow excess moisture to cook off, which will provide a thicker sauce.

5. Then you cook on high for about 4 hours or low for about 6 hours.

Creamy Paleo Cashew Curry Cauliflower

Ingredients:

1 large head of cauliflower florets (8 to 12 cups)

2 tablespoons of coconut oil

1cup of sunflower seed butter (or cashew butter)

2 to 4 tablespoons of curry powder of choice (I suggest you start with less as you can always add more)

Deep pot or stockpot (at least 8 to 12 quarts)

2 can of coconut milk (preferably, light or regular)

1cup of cashew halves

2 teaspoons of chili paste

2 teaspoons of red pepper flakes

Directions:

1. First, you add your coconut oil to your pot and set head to medium.

2. At a point when oil is hot, you add your cashew pieces and stir thoroughly. Your aim here is to lightly toast them in the oil and get them to release their oils. In this case, you may have to increase your heat.

3. After which you add a few pinches of your curry powder to the cashews while toasting them.

4. After that, you add your cauliflower florets, coconut milk, curry powder, and chili paste.

5. Then you stir thoroughly and bring your coconut milk to a light simmer.

6. Furthermore, you back the head down and cook on medium for up to 10 minutes, until cauliflower is tender and sauce has reduced slightly.

7. After which you add your sunflower or cashew butter and stir thoroughly.

8. After that, you cook until sauce is desired consistency from reduction.

9. Finally, you garnish with additional chopped cashews and red pepper flakes.

Paleo Kielbasa & Super Kraut Recipe

Tips:

This recipe takes 5 minute to prepare, while you allow the Crockpot to handle the rest.

Ingredients:

½ of one medium red cabbage head, shredded

1 large bag of Sauerkraut (about 2 pounds)

1 to 1 ½ pounds of Beef Kielbasa (sliced into ½ ″ or 1″ pieces)

Directions:

1. First, you pour the sauerkraut into your crock-pot / slow cooker, including the juices.

2. After which you add the shredded red cabbage and mix evenly into the sauerkraut.

3. After that, you cut the kielbasa into 1/2″ to 1″ lengths.

4. At this point, you place the kielbasa (cut sides up) around the edges of the crock-pot to form a ring.

5. Furthermore, you use the excess kielbasa slices to start a second ring inside of the first.

6. Then you cover your crock-pot / slow cooker and cook on low for about 4 to 5 hours.

7. Finally, you serve and package the leftovers for tomorrow or the next day.

SLOW COOKER VINDALOO WITH BEEF, PORK, CHICKEN, GOAT, OR LAMB

INGREDIENTS

6 fresh gingers (grated)

6 tablespoons mustard seeds (or grainy mustard)

3 teaspoons of cardamom

¼ teaspoon of red pepper flakes (more to taste)

1 cup of white wine vinegar (or apple cider vinegar)

2 very large onions (sliced)

2 pounds (about 4 cups) stewed (or diced tomatoes)

2 teaspoons of sea salt

Chopped parsley or cilantro (for serving)

24 cloves garlic

4 tablespoons of curry powder

3 tablespoons of cumin

1teaspoon of ground cloves

½ cup of olive oil

4 pounds of pork loin or pork shoulder, cubed (you can substitute for beef, lamb, chicken, or goat)

4 red peppers, sliced into strips (it is optional)

2 cinnamon stick

Rice (jasmine, sprouted, or basmati), for serving

Directions:

1. First, you use a blender to grind the garlic, ginger, spices, olive oil, and vinegar into a paste and if paste is too thick to process, I suggest you add a small amount of water or olive oil.

2. After which you cover the bottom of the slow cooker with the sliced onions and peppers.

3. After that, you place the cubed pork on top of the onions, and then spread the vinegar-spice paste on top of the pork.

4. At a point, you add the tomatoes, cinnamon stick, and salt.

5. Then you cook on low for about 7-8 hours or on high for 4-5 hours.

6. Finally, you serve over rice topped with fresh chopped cilantro.

Asian Slow Cooked Pork

Ingredients

1 cup of chicken stock

1cup of rice wine vinegar, plus 2 teaspoons

2 thumb size ginger knob (grated)

2 teaspoons of red pepper flakes

1 teaspoons of Chinese Five Spice

2 lbs. of mustard greens, stemmed and julienned 2" (or kale)

4-6 lbs. of Boston butt pastured pork

1 cup of Tamari (preferably, gluten free soy sauce)

8-10 cloves minced garlic, plus 2 cloves

4 tablespoons of fresh squeezed orange juice

2 teaspoons of sesame oil

Salt and pepper, to taste

2 (8 oz.) mushrooms, sliced

Directions:

1. First, you pour all of the liquid ingredients, red pepper flakes, Chinese 5 Spice, garlic, and ginger into the crock-pot.

2. After which you salt and pepper your Boston butt pork on both sides, and then add it to the crock-pot mixture as well.

3. After that, you cook on low for about 7 hours and then remove the pork.

4. At this point, you add the sliced mushrooms to the crock-pot and shred the pork on a plate.

5. Then you mix the pork back in the pot and cook for about 2 more hours.

6. Boil the mustard greens in a pot of water for about 10 minutes, right before serving.

7. Furthermore, you sauté them in a sauce pan with 2 tablespoons of rice vinegar and 2 clove of minced garlic.

8. Finally, you add the greens to the crock-pot and serve.

Healing Cuisine BBQ Meatballs

Ingredients:

2 free range organic egg

4-8 cloves garlic (minced)

A few cracks of fresh pepper, to taste

5 cups of Healing Cuisine Barbecue Sauce

4 pounds of grass fed ground beef

2 yellow onions (minced)

2 pinches of sea salt

2/3 cup of finely ground almonds (it is optional)

Directions:

1. First, you combine beef, egg, onion, garlic, optional almonds, salt and pepper in a large bowl.

2. After which you mix with your fingers.

3. After that, you shape into balls of uniform sizes (I prefer doing bite size for parties so easier to eat).

4. At this point, you heat a Tablespoon or two of coconut oil in a large skillet over Medium heat.

5. Then you add half of meatballs to pan (please do not overcrowd!) and brown on all sides.

6. After which you transport meatballs to a 6-quart pot over Medium-Low heat.

7. Brown remaining meatballs in skillet, and then you transfer to a 6-quart pot.

8. Finally, you pour Healing Cuisine Barbecue Sauce over top and simmer for about 15-20 minutes or until cooked thru.

Chicken Hearts Stroganoff (Slow Cooker Version)

Notes

1. You start by slicing the chicken hearts in thirds and then add about 10 minutes to the prep time.

2. I prefer Greek Yogurt to thicken the sauce because I like the taste and it is readily available.

3. You can also use Crème fraiche or sour cream, because they also work just as well.

4. I suggest you serve this over a bed of garlic-roasted potatoes and a side of steamed veggies.

Ingredients

2lbs. of whole mushrooms (quartered or sliced)

8 cloves garlic (minced)

2 Teaspoons of salt

1 Tablespoon of paprika

2 Cups of chicken stock

2 (7 oz.) full fat Greek yogurt

2 onions (thinly sliced)

4lbs chicken hearts (cut lengthwise in to thirds)

2 Tablespoons of Dijon mustard

2 Teaspoons of pepper

1 Tablespoon of cayenne pepper

½ Cup of heavy cream or coconut milk

Directions:

1. First, you add the onions and mushrooms to your crock-pot.

2. After which you put the chicken hearts on top but not touching the sides.

3. After that, you add the mustard, garlic, and spices.

4. At this point, you pour in the chicken stock.

5. Then you cover and cook on low for about 6 hours.

6. This is when you turn the heat off, wait about 5 minutes, and then stir in the cream and yogurt.

7. Finally, you allow sitting for about 5 to 10 more minutes and then serving.

CROCK POT CASHEW CHICKEN

INGREDIENTS

1 cup of soy sauce

½ cup of ketchup

4 cloves garlic (minced)

½ teaspoon of red pepper flakes

½ cup of water

4 pounds boneless, skinless chicken thighs

½ cup of rice vinegar

4 tablespoons of brown sugar

2 teaspoons of fresh ginger, grated

1 cup of cashews

4 tablespoons of cornstarch

Directions:

1. First, you place chicken in crock-pot.

2. After which you combine soy sauce, vinegar, ketchup, sugar, garlic, ginger, and pepper flakes in small bowl.

3. After that, you mix well and pour over chicken.

4. Then you cook on low for about 3 to 4 hours or more.

5. When it is about 30 minutes before serving, you combine the water and cornstarch and add to the chicken.

6. At this point, you stir well and then let the sauce thicken for the remainder of the cooking time.

7. Finally, you add cashews and stir just before serving.

8. Make sure you serve over rice.

Crockpot Chicken de Provence

Ingredients:

60 button mushrooms

2 Family packs of chicken thighs, remove skin (feel free to substitute with chicken breasts, drumsticks or pork chops)

2 dashes of sea salt and pepper, to taste

4 extra-large handfuls of Okra

8 tablespoons of minced garlic

2 jar of marinara sauce (or large can of tomato sauce)

6 tablespoons of herbs de Provence

Directions:

1. First, you place chicken thighs at the bottom of the Crockpot.

2. After which you season with salt and pepper.

3. After that, you cut the tops of the okra, put them in the Crockpot and sprinkle the okra with garlic.

4. At this point, you throw the mushrooms on top of the okra.

5. Then you pour your favorite clean marinara sauce on everything.

6. This is when you sprinkle the herbs de Provence on top.

7. Finally, when you done you put the Crockpot on low for about 8 hours or high for 4.

Slow Cooker Apricot Chicken

Ingredients:

6 cloves garlic (minced)

Sea salt and pepper to taste

3 lbs. boneless skinless chicken breasts and/or thighs

2 (2-inch) pieces of ginger, grated

2 cups of chicken broth (preferably homemade)

4 teaspoons of coconut oil

1 teaspoon of cinnamon

1 ¼ cups of unsweetened, un sulphered dried apricots, halved

2 large onions (chopped)

¼ teaspoon of allspice

2 (14.5 oz.) can no salt added diced tomatoes

Directions:

1. First, you melt the 2 teaspoons of the coconut oil in a pan over medium heat.

2. After which you season the chicken with sea salt and pepper, and add to the pan.

3. After that, you brown on both sides for a couple minutes, then remove from heat, and set aside.

4. Then you use the same pan to melt the remaining 2 teaspoons of coconut oil (feel free to add more if needed).

5. Furthermore, you add the onion and sauté a few minutes, until it becomes translucent.

6. After which you stir in the ginger, garlic, cinnamon and allspice and cook and stir for 30 seconds, or until fragrant.

7. After that, you add the tomatoes and chicken broth and cook a few minutes longer, until heated through.

8. This is when you pour mixture into slow cooker and add the dried halved apricots.

9. Then you place chicken on top of the mixture and cover.

10. In addition, you cook on low for approximately 5-6 hours or on high for about 3-4.

11. At this point, when it is done, shred the chicken with two forks and mix.

12. Finally, you serve a top vegetable of choice (kale, winter squash, etc.). I prefer mashed butternut squash.

Slow Cooker Creamy Italian Chicken

Ingredients

2(14.5 oz.) can diced tomatoes (or approx. 3 cups freshly diced)

2 teaspoons of basil

4-6 cloves fresh garlic (chopped)

2 cups of sliced mushrooms

½ cup of Parmesan cheese (omit for dairy free)

2 lbs. of boneless chicken breast (or thighs-pasture raised preferred)

2 cups of heavy cream or coconut milk (dairy free)

2 teaspoons of oregano

1 teaspoon of unrefined sea salt (feel free to add more to taste)

2 cups of onion (chopped)

Directions:

1. First, you spray crock with olive oil.

2. After which you add chicken, diced tomatoes, basil, oregano, garlic, salt, onions and mushrooms.

3. After that, you cook on low for about 6-7 hours or high for about 4 hours.

4. Then when it is an hour before you finished cooking, you add the cream and Parmesan cheese and mix well.

5. Finally, you serve over whole wheat, brown rice (gluten free) or fresh zucchini pasta (grain free)

CROCK POT SWISS STEAK

INGREDIENTS

½ cup of Arrowroot Starch

2 teaspoons of Sage

4 teaspoons of Salt

8 Carrots (peeled)

2 Medium Onion (sliced)

6 cups of Crushed Tomatoes (or preferably one 28 oz. can)

4 Tablespoons of Cooking Fat (lard, coconut oil, or ghee)

4 lbs. of Beef Round

4 teaspoons of Mustard Powder

2 teaspoons of Thyme Leaves

1 teaspoon of Black Pepper

8 Celery Stalks

6 Garlic Cloves (minced)

6 Tablespoons of Worcestershire Sauce

Directions:

1. First, you cut the beef into large pieces, about 3" cubes.

2. After which you combine the arrowroot starch and spices.

3. After that, you cut the carrots and celery into 3" long pieces and heat the cooking fat in a frying pan.

4. At this point, you coat the beef pieces with the spiced powder and pan fry until brown.

5. Then you transfer the meat into the crock-pot and add the carrots, celery, onions and garlic to the fry pan and then stir-fry for about 2-3 minutes until onions are mostly translucent.

6. This is when you transfer the vegetables to the crock-pot and turn off the heat in the frying pan.

7. After which you add the tomatoes and Worcestershire sauce to the frying pan to deglaze the leftover bits.

8. Then you transfer it all into the crock-pot.

9. Finally, you cover the crock-pot and cook on low for at least 8 hours.

Slow-Cooker Korean-Style Beef Short Ribs

Ingredients:

2 onions (thinly sliced)

4-inch knob of fresh ginger (sliced)

1 rice wine vinegar

2 teaspoons of red pepper flake

Sea salt and pepper to taste

6 pounds of grass fed beef short ribs

6 cloves of garlic (minced)

1 cup of organic wheat free tamari (soy sauce or coconut amino)

½ cup of raw honey

4 teaspoons of sesame oil

1 cup of chopped scallion

Directions:

1. First, you mix the tamari, rice wine vinegar and honey in the bottom of your slow cooker.

2. After which you add the sliced onion, garlic, ginger and red pepper flake to the slow cooker.

3. After that, you season your short ribs with sea salt and pepper.

4. At this point, you place them in the slow cooker and cook on high for about 3-4 hours or low for 6-8 hours.

5. At a point when the short ribs are cooked, you remove the bones and shred the beef.

6. Then you add it back into the slow cooker.

7. Finally, you stir in the sesame oil, taste and season if necessary.

8. After which you garnish with chopped scallion and serve.

Roasted Red Pepper Sweet Potato Soup

Ingredients:

2 (14 ounce) jar of roasted red peppers in water, drained

2 cups of chicken stock

4 cloves garlic

1 teaspoon of red pepper flakes

4 huge sweet potatoes (peeled and cubed, measured this is about 12 cups of cubes)

2 (14 ounce) can of coconut milk, I prefer TJ's light brand as usual

2 small yellow onions (large dice)

1 teaspoons of black pepper.

Directions:

1. First, you dump the entire ingredients into the slow cooker.

2. After which you let it cook for about 4 to 6 hours.

3. After that, you blend it with an immersion blender, food processor, or blender.

4. For me I chose not to blend it all the way to leave some chunks of potato.

5. At this point, you eat it and feel smart and good at cooking.

6. Finally, you garnish it with red pepper flakes or chipotle flakes if you so wished.

Slow Cooker Super-Fast Meatloaf

Ingredients:

3 eggs (beaten)

¾ of a small white onion (small dice)

3 stacks of celery (sliced thinly or chopped)

1 ½ teaspoons of black pepper

3 teaspoons of garlic powder

3 pounds of lean ground meat (remember that ground chicken works really well for this, as would lean turkey).

6 ounces of bacon (crisped and chopped)

6 green onions (chopped)

3 teaspoons of dried oregano

1 ½ teaspoons of thyme

3 teaspoons of smoked paprika

Ingredients for the Tomato Sauce:

3 to 4 ½ tablespoons of Dijon mustard

1 ½ teaspoons of apple cider vinegar.

1 ½ small can of tomato paste (feel free to use ½ cup of tomato sauce)

2 teaspoons of smoked paprika

3 teaspoons of garlic powder

Directions:

1. First, you cook your bacon until brown and crispy, and then chop up really good.

2. After which you combine your ground meat, beaten eggs, bacon, veggies in a large bowl and season.

3. After that, you mix the entire mixture by hand, forming a loaf.

4. At this point, you place your loaf in your slow cooker.

5. After which you press it down so that the top is flat and you have about an inch of space between the loaf and the sides of the slow cooker.

6. Then you mix your tomato sauce ingredients together and spoon them over the loaf.

7. This is the point when you use a spoon or a knife to frost the loaf's top as evenly as possible.

8. Finally, you cook on low for about 4 to 6 hours.

Slow Cooker Chicken Roll-Ups with Prosciutto and Asparagus

Ingredients:

12 to 16 slices of Prosciutto or spiced ham of choice (usually about a ½ pound will do)

Salt and Pepper to taste

6 or 8 boneless chicken breasts

2 bunches of asparagus

Garlic cloves

Directions:

1. First, filet your chicken breasts in ½.

2. After which you mash your chicken flat with a meat maillot or rather using a piece of saran wrap between the chicken and mallet helps.

3. You should smash the chicken on both sides until it is tenderized and ready to roll.

4. After that, you trim your asparagus spears to your desired length for your rolls.

5. Remember that cutting off about ½ the stalk usually works fine.

6. At this point, you place 6 to 8 pieces of asparagus along with 2 chopped cloves of garlic inside your chicken.

7. Then you proceed to roll up the chicken around the asparagus.

8. Furthermore, you roll a piece of Prosciutto or ham around your chicken roll up and you are ready to go. Make use of a wooden toothpick to hold your roll together is optional and is normally only necessary if you made a rather messy roll-up. By so doing everything will bind together nicely in the cooking stages.

10. Finally, you line the bottom of your slow cooker with the roll-ups and cook on low for about 4 hours.

Paleo Refried Beans (Delicata Squash)

Ingredients:

2 cups of sun dried tomatoes

2 cups of water

2 teaspoons of cayenne pepper

Sea salt and black pepper to taste

4 medium delicata squashes (peeled, seeded, and diced)

2 tablespoons of tomato paste

4 teaspoons of cumin

2 teaspoons of chili powder

2 teaspoons of garlic powder

Directions for crock-pot:

1. First, you soak your sun-dried tomatoes in your water for at least an hour.

2. After which you add your squash, tomato paste, sun dried tomatoes and soaking water to your crock-pot / slow cooker.

3. At this point, you add all spices and stir.

4. Then you cook on low for about 3 hours max after which you blend with an immersion blender, standard blender, or mash with a potato masher.

5. You should not puree finely, if you want a thicker consistency.

6. If mixture is not as thick as you want it, I suggest you transfer to a saucepan.

7. Furthermore, you heat on your stovetop on medium heat and reduce until it attains a desired consistency.

Super Easy Crock Pot Spaghetti Squash Curry

Ingredients:

2 cans of coconut milk (room temperature, well shaken)

8 to 12 whole garlic cloves (it is optional)

2 medium spaghetti squash (about 6 to 8 pounds)

½ cup of water (if you using a full-fat coconut milk)

2 to 4 Tablespoons of red curry paste (preferably the Paleo friendly Thai Kitchen red curry paste).

Directions:

1. First, you cut your spaghetti squash in ½ the short way (A serrated knife helps).

2. After which you scoop out the seeds from the inside of your squash halves (I advise you save them to oven roast them)

3. After that, you poke holes into the tops of your squash halves with a fork, at about 4 different points.

4. At this point, you pour your coconut milk (and water i.e. if you using full fat coconut milk) into your crock-pot, and add your curry paste (and the garlic cloves if you are using them).

5. Then you mix your curry paste into your coconut milk until it dissolved.

6. Furthermore, you place your squash halves open/cut side down into your coconut curry mixture.

7. After which you cover and cook on low for about 4 to 5 hours.

8. After that, you remove your squash halves from your crock-pot (be careful it will be hot!) and use a large fork to scoop them out into a large bowl.

9. At this point when your squash is removed into a bowl, you add as much or as little of the coconut curry mixture remaining in your slow cooker and stir well.

10. If you included garlic cloves, I suggest you mash them up and mix them in well.

11. Finally, you garnish with fresh cilantro and serve.

Slow Cooker Red & Yellow Pepper

Ingredients:

3 medium to large bell peppers, diced (Note: for a sweeter sauce, I suggest you use 2 yellow and 1 red, Vice versa for less sweetness)

6 to 8 cloves of garlic (cut in ½ and tossed right in)

Salt to taste

6 to 7 cups of BPA-free crushed tomatoes (or 3 ½ to 4 pounds of fresh tomatoes, blanched and peeled)

One medium to large white onion (diced)

2 tablespoons of extra virgin olive oil

One tablespoon of Italian seasoning (or 1 teaspoon each basil, oregano, and thyme)

Note:

This recipe is designed for a 6-quart slow cooker, but if you using a 4-quart model, I suggest you use 2/3 of the ingredient amounts.

Directions:

1. First, you add your tomatoes and olive oil to your slow cooker (if you are using fresh tomatoes, I suggest you mash them up in the crock).

2. After which you stir in your seasonings, garlic, onion, and peppers.

3. After that, you cook on low for about 5 hours or high for 3 hours.

4. At this point, you use your immersion blender to achieve an even consistency, or blend less if you desire a chunkier sauce.

5. In the other hand, if you do not have an immersion blender, feel free to use your food processor or blender.

6. Then you serve over steamed or sautéed zucchini ribbons or noodles made with your spiral slicer.

7. Finally, you serve and make sure you freeze any extra sauce you don't think you'll use in

8. The next few days!

Cinnamon & Cayenne Sweet Potatoes and Apples

Ingredients:

4 gala apples (Peeled, cored, and sliced medium)

2 to 4 teaspoons of cayenne pepper

Slight pinches of finely ground sea salt

8 cups of sweet potatoes (sliced medium thin)

4 tablespoons of ghee (or coconut oil)

1 teaspoon of ground cumin

2 to 4 teaspoons of ground cinnamon

Directions:

1. First, you peel and slice your sweet potatoes into medium thin slices (I prefer using a mandolin)

2. After which you peel and core your apples, and slice them into the same thickness.

3. After that, you layer your apples and potatoes in your slow cooker, mixing the apples among the potatoes.

4. At this point, you add your seasonings and mix well either by hand or with a spoon, making sure everything is coated evenly.

5. This is when you add your coconut oil or ghee to the top so it melts down during cooking.

6. Then you cook on high for about 3 hours or low for 6.

7. Finally, you result will be somewhat mushy and brown, yet super easy and super tasty.

Saratoga Chips

Ingredients:

4-6 tablespoons of olive oil

2 teaspoons of cumin

2 teaspoons of ground black pepper

6-8 baking potatoes (sliced thin, skin on with a mandolin ~1/4" or thinner

2-4 tablespoons of echili powder

2 teaspoons of salt

Directions:

1. Meanwhile, you heat oven to a temperature of 450 deg.

2. After which you mix potatoes oil and spices until they're all covered with spice mixture (I prefer to use a zip top bag to do this).

3. After that, you grease two cookie sheets with olive oil and place chips on a single layer.

4. At this point, you bake until chips are crispy for about 30 – 40 min (try to check occasionally and it also depends on your pans and ovens and the thickness of the chips you may need to turn them).

5. Feel free to also fry and add the seasonings at the end.

Easy Crock Pot "Rotisserie Style" Chicken

Spice Rub (I suggest you play with your favorites)

You blend the following together:

2 teaspoons of garlic powder

2 teaspoons of dried oregano (I prefer thyme and rosemary, because work well too as does a blend of all)

2 teaspoons of paprika (I suggest smoked or half-and-half add a nice touch)

3 teaspoons of kosher salt (I suggest you use less for finer-grain salt)

2 teaspoons of onion powder

2 teaspoons of chili powder (I prefer anchco but a blended chili powder works too)

2 teaspoons of fresh ground black pepper to taste

Ingredient for the Chicken

4-6 carrots (scrubbed, topped and tailed and cut into 3" lengths)

4 small onions (quartered)

4-40 cloves of garlic (it is optional)

2 (3-4 lbs.) bird

4-6 ribs celery, scrubbed (cut into 3" lengths)

2 lemon pierced (it is optional)

Directions:

In a large Crock Pot, (I prefer the oval shaped):

1. First, you put carrots, celery, and one of the onions on the bottom along with any of the organ meats and neck that may have come with the chicken.

2. After which you tuck chicken wing tips back.

3. After that, you stuff onion and optional lemon and garlic in center cavity of chicken.

4. At this point, you place chicken into crock-pot on top of veggies.

5. Then you rub bird with olive oil.

6. This is when you cover bird with all of spice blend.

7. Finally, you put lid on crock-pot and set on high for about 5 hours.

Crockpot Chicken Tacos

Tips:

Feel free to use any toppings of your choice for your tacos, so you are free to branch out from what I used.

Ingredients

1 teaspoon of salt

2 teaspoons of chili powder

1 teaspoon of smoked paprika

½ teaspoon of cayenne powder (feel free to use more or less, depending on how hot you like it)

2 Jar of Salsa (feel free to use you choose your favorite kind)

Juice of 2 limes

8 organic free-range chicken breasts

1 teaspoon of pepper

2 teaspoons of cumin

1 teaspoon of garlic powder

½ teaspoon of oregano

2-pablano pepper (finely diced)

Ingredients for the taco Toppings

2 tomatoes (diced)

2 cups of cheddar cheese, shredded (use goat cheese for a cow's dairy-free version)

Fresh cilantro (to top the tacos)

Lettuce leaves, for the taco shells (use any of your choice)

2 avocados (sliced)

2/3 cup of onion (diced)

Sour cream, it is optional (you can omit if you avoiding dairy)

Kind of lettuce, I suggest you stay away from iceberg; it is never the best choice.

Directions

1. First, you place the chicken breasts flat in the Crockpot.

2. After which you top with all of the spices, evenly distributed over each chicken breast.

3. I suggest you measure all of the spices into a bowl, mix them together, and feel free to sprinkle them individually over the chicken breasts.

4. At this point, when the spices are on the chicken, dump a jar of salsa evenly over the chicken breasts and top with the diced poblano pepper and lime juice.

5. Then you set your Crockpot for about 4 or 8 hours (high or low) depending on when you want to eat the chicken.

6. At this point when the chicken is done, you take two forks and pull the chicken apart so it is shredded.

7. Furthermore, you mix (all the salsa and sauce together) making sure that everything is mixed well.

8. After which you put all of your toppings on a serving plate or little bowls so you can easily grab them while assembling your tacos.

9. Finally, you serve and eat as many lettuces wrap tacos as you wish (feel free to make into taco salad too if you wish)

Crock Pot Roasted Chicken Recipe

Tips:

This recipe is quick, easy, nutritious and delicious.

Ingredients

2 onions (white or yellow)

2 teaspoons of Thyme

2 teaspoons of Sage

1 teaspoons of Pepper

2 whole chicken (I suggest you remove giblets, neck, and use for stock)

12-16 cloves garlic (sub 2-4 Tablespoons Garlic Powder)

2 teaspoons of Rosemary

2 teaspoons of Tarragon

1 teaspoon of Salt

Directions:

1. First, you remove the chicken from the package, removing neck and giblets for use in stock and rinse chicken in cold water.

2. After which you roughly chop onion and stuff it into the cavity of the chicken.

3. After that, you slice garlic cloves and insert between the skin and the meat of the chicken.

4. At this point, you combine seasoning and rub onto the chicken.

5. Then you place everything in the Crock-pot on high for about 4-6 hours.

Note: make sure you cook for 4 hours, because the longer it cooks the more tender it will be.

6. Then you throw in veggies of your choice when you are cooking then dinner is done.

Easy Slow Cooker Cuban Ropa Viejas

Ingredients

4 bell peppers (use any color of your choice)

2 (26.46 oz.) box Pomi chopped tomatoes

4-8 bay leaves

2 tablespoons of cumin

Black pepper, to taste

4-8 lbs. grass-fed beef (preferably, chuck roast, brisket, or flank steak)

2 onions (white or yellow)

½ -1 head garlic, pressed (or finely minced)

1 tablespoon of dried oregano

Sea salt

Directions:

1. First, you coarsely chop the peppers, onion, and press or mince the garlic.

2. After which you add the entire ingredients (except the beef) to the slow cooker and gently stir to combine.

3. After that, you place beef on top and cook on low for about 8-10 hours.

4. Note that the meat is done when it is easily shredded with a fork.

5. Then you leave meat in the slow cooker and carefully shred it (be careful so you do not splash yourself or your walls!) and mix with the sauce.

6. At this point, you remove bay leaves and discard.

7. After which you garnish with fresh chopped cilantro.

8. This recipe can be eaten alone as a hearty stew or served with a number of sides which includes white rice, cauliflower rice, plantains (or either sweet platanos maduros or savory tostones), or even sweet potatoes or beets.

Savory Slow Cooker Chuck Roast & Butternut Squash Combo Meal

Ingredients:

4 to 6 pounds of butternut squash (halved and seeded)

8 cloves of garlic (cut in half)

2 teaspoons of paprika

Sea salt to taste

6 to 10 pounds' chuck roast

2 (8-ounce) can of fire roasted tomatoes, diced or pureed

2 teaspoons of cumin

Some teaspoon of Black pepper

4 teaspoons of onion powder

Directions:

1. First, you cut your squash in half lengthwise and scoop out the seeds.

2. After which you use a knife to poke 8 scattered holes into your chuck roast, and then stick the garlic clove halves in.

3. After that, you mix (all of your spices together) and apply the rub evenly to the chuck roast.

4. At this point, you place your chuck roast in your slow cooker and cover it with you can of fire-roasted tomatoes.

5. Then you place your squash halves in skin side down, cut side facing up, as in the picture above.

6. Furthermore, you cook on low for about 6 hours.

7. After which you carefully use a large fork to scoop the squash out and mash it.

8. Finally, you either slice or shred your beef with forks, and then serve.

Coconut milk curry beef stew crock pot recipe

INGREDIENTS

4 pounds of stewing beef (cut to about 2" cubes)

4 cups of chopped onion (4 medium onions)

4 cups of chopped carrots (4 medium carrots)

3 cups of chopped sweet potato (2 medium sweet potatoes)

2 cups of coconut milk

Salt to taste

4 tablespoons of coconut oil

½ teaspoons of salt

4 cups of chopped celery (4 stalks)

4 cups of chopped parsnips (6 small parsnips)

6 cups of bone broth

2 tablespoons of curry powder (for AIP use 2 tablespoons of turmeric)

Directions:

1. First, you heat coconut oil in a large pan over medium- high heat.

2. After which you brown the stewing beef, be careful not to overcrowd the pan.

3. After that, you sprinkle about ½ teaspoons of salt over the beef as it cooks.

4. At this point, the beef just needs to be lightly seared and not fully cooked.

5. Once it browned on all sides, you transfer the beef pieces into the crock-pot.

6. Furthermore, you add onions and celery to the same pan that the beef was cooked in.

7. After which you brown the onions and celery for about five minutes and then add them to the crock-pot.

8. After that, you add the chopped carrots, parsnips and sweet potato to the crock-pot.

9. Mix the bone broth, coconut milk and curry powder in a small bowl.

10. Then you pour this mixture over the contents of the crock-pot and cover and cook on the low setting of the crock-pot for about 8 hours, or on the high setting for 4 hours.

11. Finally, when it done, salt to taste and serve.

Rosemary Lemon Garlic Lamb with Sweet Potato Noodles

Tips:

Remember to save the bone from your leg of lamb that you can freeze and then use to make lamb stock.

Ingredients

6-8 stalks of fresh rosemary

Zest & juice of 2 lemons

4 medium sweet potatoes

4 tablespoons of olive oil

2-4 Tablespoons of flat leaf parsley, for garnish

1 leg of lamb

6-8 garlic cloves (peeled)

½ cup of liquid (either water or broth)

2-4 Tablespoons of ghee (or coconut oil)

Sea salt and black pepper, to taste

Directions:

1. First, you place your half leg of lamb fat side up onto a chopping board.

2. After which you use a sharp knife score the fat on top of the lamb in a crosshatch form.

3. After that, you season the lamb all over with sea salt & cracked black pepper.

4. At this point, you remove the rosemary from the stalk and add to a food processor, along with your lemon zest and garlic cloves.

5. Then you process until mixed then slowly drizzle in your olive oil.

6. Furthermore, you spread the paste all over the lamb, making sure to get the paste into the places you scored with your knife.

7. After which you place lamb in your slow cooker, then pour over ½ cup of liquid, and squeeze over the juice of the lemon your zester.

8. After that, you place on low heat and allow cooking for about 6-8 hours.

9. Finally, once it is ready, you carefully remove to a chopping board and let rest for 10 minute before slicing/shredding.

Directions for the sweet potato noodles

1. First, you peel your sweet potatoes and then cut each one in thirds.

2. After which you use a spiralizer or a julienne peeler to create "noodle" strands.

3. At a point when your noodles are ready, you add your butter/ghee into a skillet and place on medium heat.

4. Then once melted, you throw in your noodles and season with S&P.

5. After that, you toss to coat and cook until softened.

6. Finally, you serve with some sliced slow cooked leg of lamb on top and garnish with some flat leaf parsley on top.

Apple Cranberry Mulled Cider (Slow-Cooked)

INGREDIENTS

6 cups of cranberry juice

1cup of fresh cranberries

1 large Granny Smith apple (about 1cup)

8 cinnamon sticks

¼ teaspoon of ground nutmeg

12 cups of apple juice

½ cup of honey

1 large orange, sliced (about 1 cup), plus orange peel

2 tablespoons of sliced fresh ginger (about 6-10 slices)

1 teaspoon of whole cloves (about 20-30 cloves)

½ teaspoon of ground allspice

DIRECTIONS

1. First, you pour juices in Crock Pot

2. After which you add cranberries and cinnamon sticks and then chop orange in half.

3. After that, you use a peeler or any one of your choice to peel the rind of the oranges.

4. Then you add peels to the pot and then thinly slice the orange half...

5. At this point, you thinly slice half of the apple and roughly chop some fresh ginger- about 2 tablespoons worth.

6. Furthermore, you add orange, apple, and ginger to pot.

7. After that, you add spices- allspice, nutmeg, and cloves.

8. Then you stir and taste, after which you cook on low for about 4-7 hours, remember that the longer you cook it, the more potent the spices will become.

9. At a point when done, you serve up what you want and then you can jar any extra cider to have later.

10. Feel free to serve hot or cold.

Crock-Pot Chicken Tortilla Soup

Ingredients:

2 (15-ounce) can whole peeled tomatoes (mashed)

2 Anaheim chili or 2 (4-ounce) can chopped green Chile peppers

8 cups of chicken stock

2 teaspoons of chili powder

½ teaspoons of black pepper

Shredded, cooked chicken (it is optional)

2 onions (diced)

4 cloves garlic (pressed)

2 teaspoons of cumin

2 teaspoons of salt

14 corn tortillas

Oil

Directions:

1. First, you place chicken, tomatoes, onion, green chilies, and garlic into a slow cooker.

2. After which you pour in stock and season with spices.

3. After that, you cover, and cook on Low for about 6-8 hours.

4. Meanwhile, you heat oven to a temperature of 400 degrees.

5. At this point, you brush both sides of tortillas lightly with oil.

6. Then you cut tortillas into strips, and then spread on a baking sheet.

7. Finally, you bake until crisp, about 10 minutes.

8. Before you serve, sprinkle tortilla strips over soup.

9. Then garnish with grated cheese, avocado, sour cream and lime juice.

Coconut Green Chili Chicken Soup (dairy and gluten free)

Ingredients

12 carrots, chopped into bite-sized pieces

2 cups of diced mild green chilies

2 teaspoons of granulated garlic

1 teaspoon of cumin powder

½ teaspoon of fresh ground black pepper

2 cups of coconut milk or coconut cream

Lime (for serving)

4 pounds of organic chicken breasts or thighs (chopped into bite-sized pieces)

2 medium white onions (diced)

2-quart chicken stock (preferably, homemade)

2 teaspoons of sea salt

1 teaspoon of coriander powder

4-6 tablespoons of coconut flour

Cilantro (for serving)

Directions:

1. First, you dice your chicken into bite-sized pieces and place in crock-pot.

2. After which you dice your onion and carrots and add to chicken.

3. After that, you add the diced green chilies, garlic, salt, chicken stock, cumin, coriander, and black pepper to crock-pot.

4. At this point, you stir until well combined.

5. Then you cover and cook on low for about 5 hours and about 10 minutes before serving, stir in your coconut milk or cream and the coconut flour.

6. **Note** that the coconut flour will help thicken the soup just a bit.

7. Finally, you taste for salt and adjust as needed.

8. After which you garnish with fresh cilantro and a splash of lime juice.

Slow Cooker Baked Apple Recipe

Ingredients:

½ cup of raisins

12 tablespoons of coconut oil, butter, or ghee

12 medium to large green apples

½ cup of honey

2 teaspoons of cinnamon

Directions:

Directions on how to core apples.

1. First, you use an apple corer or paring knife, cut around the core (about ¼ inches from the stem all the way around) but leave about half an inch at the bottom.

2. After which you use the knife to 'drill out' the core.

3. After that, you divide raisins, honey, cinnamon, and coconut oil between the apples.

4. At this point, you place apples in a crock-pot and add ½ inch of water.

5. Then you cook on low overnight and enjoy in the morning!

6. In the other way round, you can bake covered at 350 degrees in a glass dish for about 45 minutes-1 hour in the morning.

7. Finally, you top with cream, yogurt, coconut milk, or just eat plain.

Homemade Slow Cooker Hot Chocolate

Ingredients:

½ teaspoon of sea salt

2 cups of heavy cream

6 tablespoons of maple syrup

4 ounces of pure chocolate of your choice

¼ cup of shaved chocolate

½ cup of cocoa powder

6 cups of whole milk

1 teaspoon of vanilla extract

4 tablespoons of cinnamon

2 cups of whipped cream

2 ounces of this and 2 ounces of this is suggested for a rich and healthy hot chocolate

Directions:

1. First, you whisk the cocoa, salt and milk all in a medium bowl.

2. After which you pour mixture into a slow cooker and add vanilla.

3. After that, you cover and cook on low for about 2 hours.

4. At this point, you add cream, cinnamon and maple syrup.

5. Then you cover, and cook on low for an additional 20 minutes.

6. This is when you stir in 2 ounces of chocolate until melted.

7. Note that it will be best to break or shave chocolate into smaller pieces before you add to the slow cooker to help in the melting process.

8. Furthermore, you pour hot chocolate into mugs and top with whipped cream and a teaspoon of shaved chocolate.

9. Finally, you grab a mug, get warm and enjoy the time with your family.

Best BBQ Crock Pot Chicken

Ingredients

2 white onions (sliced)

2 teaspoons of sea salt

2 teaspoons of dried thyme

2 teaspoons of cayenne

1 teaspoon of black pepper

2 whole chicken, giblets removed and cleaned

4 teaspoons of paprika

2 teaspoons of onion powder

2 teaspoons of white pepper

1 teaspoon of garlic powder

Directions:

1. First, you pat dry your entire chicken inside and out with paper towels.

2. After which you line the bottom of your crock-pot with the sliced onions.

3. After that, you place the chicken in your crock-pot on top of the onions.

4. At this point, you combine all remaining ingredients in a bowl and mix well.

5. Then you use your hands, rub mixture over the entire chicken, inside and out and make sure you lay it on thick and do not miss any spot.

6. Furthermore, you place the lid on your Crockpot.

7. After which you cook on low for about 6 hours or until your chicken is done.

8. Then you serve with the side of your choice.

Crock Pot Balsamic Roast

Ingredients

4 lb. of top round roast

16 ounces' tomato sauce

1 cup of water

4 tablespoons of coconut oil

Salt and Black Pepper, to taste

Garlic Powder

Balsamic Roast

2 large sweet onions (sliced)

1cup of balsamic vinegar

4 tablespoons of white wine

Rub

Smoked Paprika

Onion Powder

Directions:

1. First, you season your roast on both sides generously with the spices listed above to your desired amount.

2. After which you heat your coconut oil in a large pan over medium-high heat, and once it warm sear each side of your roast for 3-4minutes.

3. After that, you place your sliced onions in the bottom of your crock-pot and put your seared meat on top of the onions.

4. At this point, you combine your balsamic vinegar and tomato sauce in a bowl and mix thoroughly, and then pour over your meat in the crock-pot.

5. Then you add your water and white wine to your pan and de-glaze it.

6. Finally, you pour this mixture in your crock-pot as well and then place the lid on, set to low and cook for 6-8 hours.

7. After which you serve and enjoy!

Slow Cook Thai Chicken

Ingredients:

1 large red bell pepper (seeded and sliced into strips)

½ cup of chicken broth

1 tablespoon of ground cumin

½ teaspoon of red pepper flakes

2 tablespoons of cornstarch

1 tablespoon of soy sauce

3 green onions (chopped)

½ cup of peanuts, chopped roasted

6 skinless, boneless chicken breast halves (cut into ½-inch strips)

1 large onion (coarsely chopped)

¼ cup of soy sauce

3 cloves of garlic (minced)

Salt and pepper

2/3 cup of creamy peanut butter

¼ cup of lime juice

¼ cup of chopped fresh cilantro

Directions:

1. First, you place the chicken breast strips, bell pepper and onion into a slow cooker.

2. After which you pour in the chicken broth and ¼ cup of soy sauce.

3. After that, you season with cumin, garlic, red pepper flakes, salt and pepper.

4. Then you stir to blend, then cover and cook on low for about 4 ½ to 5 hours.

5. At this point, you remove 1 cup of the liquid from the slow cooker, and mix this with the cornstarch, peanut butter, 1 tablespoon of soy sauce and lime juice.

Note: it should blend into a thick sauce.

6. Then you stir the sauce back into the slow cooker, and place the lid on the pot.

7. Finally, you cook on high for about 30 minutes.

8. Before serving make sure, you garnish with green onions, cilantro and peanuts.

Italian Crock Pot Chili

Ingredients:

2 onions, chopped

2 (28oz) cans of fire-roasted diced tomatoes

6-8 tablespoons of capers

2-4 c broth or stock (I suggest you use homemade chicken broth)

4 tablespoons of dried thyme

4 tablespoons of chili powder

Salt and pepper to taste

Drizzle of olive oil

6-8 lbs. of ground beef

2 (10oz) pkg baby Bella mushrooms, diced

2 tablespoons of minced garlic (let say around 12 cloves)

½ small can of tomato paste

6 bay leaves

4 tablespoons of dried basil

2 tablespoons of cayenne (it is optional)

4-6 tablespoons of balsamic vinegar

Directions:

The best way that you can brown many ground beef is as follows:

1. First, you place all your ground beef in the crock-pot along with salt and pepper and one chopped onion.

2. After which you turn on low and cook for about 3-4 hours, stirring occasionally.

3. Remember that you can use this in SO many ways, but I prefer to drain the fat, throw the meat back in, and make chili!

4. At this point, when your meat is done, drained, you add mushrooms, garlic, tomatoes, capers, and tomato paste.

5. After that, you stir and then add the remaining ingredients and mix thoroughly.

6. Then you cook on low for about 3 or so hours or until the veggies are done to your desired level.

7. Finally, you serve with diced avocado on top or plain, both are delish!

Slow-Cooker Barbecue Ribs Recipe

Ingredients

1 ½ onion (minced)

3 ¾ cups of homemade ketchup

¾ tablespoons of smoked paprika

½ cup of honey (it is optional)

Sea salt and freshly ground black pepper to taste

6 lbs. of pork baby back ribs

1 ½ pear (peeled and diced)

1 ½ tablespoons of chili powder

3 teaspoons of dried oregano

3 tablespoons of apple cider vinegar

3 teaspoons of coconut aminos

Directions:

1. Meanwhile, you heat your oven to a temperature of 400 F.

2. After which you remove the membrane from the ribs by loosening it with a dull knife and then peeling it off.

3. After that, you season the ribs to taste on both side with sea salt and black pepper.

4. At this point, you place the ribs in a baking pan and then brown them in the oven for about 10 to 12 minutes on each side and set aside.

5. Then you combine the ketchup, onion, pear, chili powder, paprika, oregano, apple cider vinegar, coconut aminos, and honey (if using), in a bowl, and season to taste with salt and pepper.

6. Finally, you place the ribs in your slow cooker, and pour in the sauce, making sure you coat all the meat.

7. After which you cover and cook on low for about 7 to 8 hours.

Slow Cooker Queso Chicken Chili Recipe

Ingredients

4 ½ bell peppers (minced)

1 ½ jalapeño pepper, minced (it is optional)

3 garlic cloves (minced)

1 ½ teaspoons of ground cumin

Sea salt and freshly ground black pepper to taste

1 ½ lbs. of boneless skinless chicken breasts

1 ½ red onions (chopped)

3 cups of salsa

2 ½-cups of water

3 teaspoons of chili powder

2 avocados (chopped)

Directions:

1. First, you combine the chicken breasts, garlic, salsa, water, cumin, chili powder, onion, in a slow cooker, and season with salt and pepper to taste.

2. After which you cover and cook on low for about 6 to 8 hours (or on high for about 3-4 hours).

3. Once the cooking is done, you remove the chicken breasts and shred them with a fork, after which you return them to the slow cooker.

4. After that, you place the bell peppers and jalapeño in a large skillet over a high heat and cook for about 4 to 5 minutes or until well roasted.

5. Then you add the peppers and jalapeño to the slow cooker.

6. At this point, you give everything a good stir and cover.

7. After which you let the chili simmer for another 20 minutes, and add some water to reach the desired consistency, if needed.

8. Make sure you top with avocado before serving.

Slow Cooker Buffalo Chicken Meatballs Recipe

Ingredients

2/3 cup of almond meal

4 cloves garlic (minced)

1 ¼ cup of buffalo sauce

Sea salt and freshly ground black pepper to taste

2 lbs. ground chicken

2 eggs

4 green onions (thinly sliced)

Homemade ranch dressing (it is optional)

Directions:

1. Meanwhile, you heat your oven to a temperature of 400 degrees F.

2. After which you combine the ground chicken, almond meal, egg, garlic, green onions, in a bowl and season with salt and pepper to taste.

3. After that, you mix everything until well combined.

4. At this point, you roll the mixture into 1 ½ -inch meatballs.

5. Then you place the meatballs onto a baking sheet and bake for about 5 minutes in the preheated oven.

6. This is the point when you turn off the oven and place meatballs into a slow cooker.

7. Furthermore, you add the buffalo sauce, and stir to combine.

8. Then you cover and cook on low for about 2 hours.

9. Finally, you serve with ranch sauce for dipping (it is optional).

Slow Cooker Chipotle Barbacoa Brisket

Ingredients:

1 to 2 cups of my Chipotle Adobo Sauce (or 6 chipotles from a can plus 6 tablespoons of sauce)

2 small white onions (diced)

4 teaspoons of oregano

4 bay leaves

2 (2.5 to 4 pound) beef brisket

4 cups of beef stock

6 large cloves of garlic

1 teaspoon of ground cloves

2 tablespoons of apple cider vinegar

Directions:

1. First, you make a liquid puree with all of your ingredients except the beef or the bay leaves.

2. After which you pour about a quarter of your liquid puree into the bottom of your slow cooker.

3. After that, you trim any excessive fat from your brisket and place it in your slow cooker fat cap side down.

4. Remember that you do not need a lot of fat on your brisket at all.

5. At this point, you pour the rest of your liquid puree over your brisket ensuring that you coat the top sides.

6. Then you cook on low for about 8 hours.

7. Furthermore, you remove your brisket to a large bowl or container to pull/shred with 2 forks.

8. After which you add some of the cooking liquid from the crock-pot to your pulled brisket.

9. Serve in lettuce wrap tacos, with your eggs, over salads, or just by pulling strips off and feeding your face!

Slow cooked pork ribs recipe

Ingredients

10 tablespoons of homemade ketchup

4 tablespoons of apple cider vinegar

Sea salt and freshly ground black pepper to taste

6 lbs. of pork spare ribs

1 ¼ cups of water (or homemade stock)

2 teaspoons of mustard powder

4 tablespoons of Worcestershire sauce (it is optional)

Directions:

1. First, you combine the entire ingredients except for the ribs in the slow-cooker pot.

2. After which you give it a really good mix, because when you cook this way, you do not have to pause and stir; therefore, you wish to make sure the sauce is consistent and you do not get flavors in one bite that you will not get in another.

3. At a point when everything is well combined, you give the ribs a good rub with the sauce; place them in the pot, cover and cook for about 8 hours on low heat.

4. Remember that the cooking time may be long, but the reward is well worth it.

5. Make sure you serve the ribs with the cooking liquid as a sauce.

Sour Cream & Bacon Crock Pot Chicken

Ingredients

16 boneless and skinless chicken breasts

1 cup of flour

16 bacon slices

2 cups of sour cream

4 (10 oz.) cans of roasted garlic cream of mushroom soup

Directions:

This recipe can be prepared in two ways:

1. First, you place the bacon in a large skillet and then you cook over medium-low heat until some of the fat is rendered.

2. You should make sure that the bacon is still pliable and not crisp.

3. After which you drain on paper towels, and if you use this method, reduce the flour to ¼ cup or do not cook the bacon and proceed with the recipe.

4. After that, you wrap one slice of bacon around each boneless chicken breast and place in a 4 - 5-quart Crockpot.

5. At this point, you combine condensed soups, sour cream, and flour in medium bowl, and mix with wire whisk to blend.

6. Then you pour over chicken.

7. Furthermore, you cover Crockpot and cook on low for about 6 – 8 hours until chicken and bacon are thoroughly cooked.

8. This is when you remove the chicken and beat the sauce with a wire whisk so it is very well blended.

9. Finally, you pour sauce over chicken.

Crockpot Breakfast Casserole

Notes

I suggest you use a Crockpot liner sprayed with non - stick cooking spray for easy clean - up.

Ingredients

2 cups of milk

2 lbs. of sausage, browned and drained (or 2 lb. of bacon, cooked and crumbled) or use both

½ teaspoon of dry mustard (it is optional)

1 teaspoon of black pepper

2 green pepper, diced (it is optional)

2 dozen eggs

2 packages (64 oz.) of frozen hash brown potatoes

4 cups of cheddar cheese (or Colby jack, shredded)

1 teaspoon of salt

1 cup of green onions, diced (it is optional)

Directions:

1. First, you spray your Crockpot with no stick cooking spray or preferably, you use a slow cooker liner and spray it.

2. After which you layer frozen potatoes, bacon or sausage, onions (if you using), green pepper (if you using) and 2 cups of shredded cheese in the Crockpot in 2 or 3 layers.

3. After that, you sprinkle the remaining 2 cups of shredded cheese over the top evenly.

4. At this point, you beat the eggs, milk, dry mustard, salt and pepper together.

5. Then you pour the eggs mixture over the cheese evenly in the Crockpot.

6. Finally, you cook on low for about 7 to 8 hours or until eggs are set and thoroughly cooked before, you serve.

Casein-Free Crockpot Frito Pie (Gluten-Free)

Ingredients

2 ½ lbs. of beef chuck roast

2 cups of water

1 teaspoons of cumin

1 teaspoons of cornstarch (gluten – free)

16 oz. of salsa

1 large onion (chopped)

1 (15 – oz.) can pinto beans (preferable, with liquid)

1 teaspoon of salt

1 teaspoons of granulated onion

¼ teaspoon of cayenne pepper

15 oz. bag Frito corn chips

Use toppings of your choice: ranging from guacamole, hot sauce, lettuce, corn, dairy – free cheese, etc.)

Directions:

1. First, you place chuck roast into Crockpot.

2. After which you combine chopped onion, beans, water, cumin, granulated onion, cornstarch, and cayenne pepper.

3. After that, you pour over top of roast in Crockpot.

4. Then you cover Crockpot and cook on LOW for about 8 - 10 hours.

5. At this point, you remove meat from Crockpot and using 2 forks, shred meat.

6. Furthermore, you drain about half the liquid from the Crockpot.

7. After that, you return shredded meat to the Crockpot and stir soybeans and juices will mix in.

8. Finally, you place Fritos in individual bowls, after which you add meat and your favorite toppings.

Crockpot Pear, Apple and Pork Dinner

Ingredients

4 pears (sliced)

2 onions (sliced)

3 c. apple juice

6 T. Mustard

6 apples (sliced)

6 lb. pork (cubed into 1 inch pieces)

3 c. brown sugar

1 c. vinegar

Directions:

If you wish to prepare it as Freezer Meal write the following instructions on the bag:

1. First, you add 5 c. water, and cook on low for about 6 - 8 hours or high for about 3 - 4 hours.

2. After which you cut up meat, fruit and onions and then place in freezer in a gallon size bag.

3. After that, you mix brown sugar, apple juice, vinegar and mustard together then pour into the bag.

4. At this point, you lay flat in freezer.

5. When it is ready to prepare, you thaw overnight in the fridge.

6. Then you pour contents into Crockpot and add 5 c. water.

7. Stir the mixture very well.

8. Finally, you cook on low for about 6 - 8 hours or high for about 3 - 4 hours.

9. Then you serve.

Conclusion

To lose weight is very easy if you know the process and how to go about it. That is the reason for this Book, to help you achieve your weight loss goal in No time. Get in shape while eating the foods you love. Take advantage of this healthy and delicious recipes provided for you in this book.

Remember, the only bad action you can take is no action at all.

www.ingramcontent.com/pod-product-compliance
Lightning Source LLC
Chambersburg PA
CBHW081725100526
44591CB00016B/2506